Wester Ross: Shorter Routes

Distance: *up to 2¹/₂ miles/4km*
Height climbed: *440m*
Difficulty: *Grade A*
Facilities: *None*

A circuit of one of Scotland's most distinctive hills, including a steep, short climb to its ridge. Paths are rough and unclear in places; the views are breathtaking.

To reach this walk, drive north from Ullapool for 10 miles on the A835 and then turn left on the narrow road to Achiltibuie. The car park is 5 miles along this road.

Stac Pollaidh consists of a steep skirt of peat and scree, rising to a short, narrow ridge between two rocky outcrops, like ruined towers. The path rises from the road and splits just before the second of two gates. Take the right-hand branch and follow it up and around the eastern end of the hill.

Just as you come round to the north side of the hill there is another junction. The right-hand path continues to traverse around the north and west flanks of the hill, prior to descending to complete a circuit by linking with the outward path below the upper gate. The left-hand path rises steeply to reach the lowest point of the ridge.

From the ridge, another path heads off north-west, keeping to the left of a fenced-off area, as it descends to join the circular path (*see* map).

Please note: there have been problems with erosion on Stac Pollaidh. In order to minimise this, you are asked to stick to the paths.

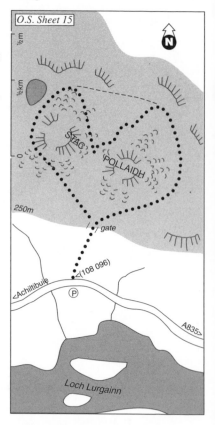

O.S. Sheet 15

Stac Pollaidh from the south-east

Distance: 6¹/₂ miles/10.5km
Height climbed: 89m (on road)
Difficulty: Grade B
Facilities: Toilets, Food (Ullapool)

A walk along the shore of Loch Broom with a possible return by the A835. The path by the loch is generally rough and stony, with some rocky outcrops to cross. Fine views of coastal scenery.

Park in Ullapool and make your way to West Terrace, overlooking Ullapool River and facing the mouth of Loch Broom. Take the path down to the river and cross the footbridge, then follow the left-hand metalled track beyond. When this turns up to the right go left on a grassy track through gorse, leading down to a cottage by the riverside then on, round the edge of the golf course (red markers), to the foreshore.

At first the going is quite easy, along a grassy verge with cultivated croft land behind the foreshore, but it gradually becomes rougher, with blocks of rock forming sea-worn barriers across the upper half of the shore. After 2¹/₂ miles the path reaches Allt an t-Srathain. If the water is low this burn can be easily forded and the shore followed on to the lighthouse; if not, it may be necessary to cut right, up to the A835, and then turn left on the minor road to Rhue. There is a footpath to the lighthouse from the end of the road. From here there are splendid views across the loch, and out towards the Summer Isles.

Return to Ullapool either back along the shore or by the A835 – though this can be busy.

View looking north-west past Rhue Lighthouse

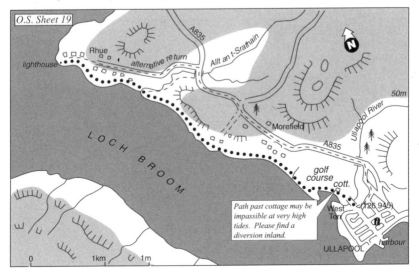

Distance: *2 miles/3km (there and back)*
Height climbed: *250m*
Difficulty: *Grade B*
Facilities: *Toilets, Food (Ullapool)*

A short, brisk hill climb leading to fine views over Ullapool, Loch Broom and the surrounding mountains. The paths are rough but clear.

Follow the A835 (North Road) north from the Ullapool foreshore and watch for the entrances to Broom Court to the right. Take the second, signposted for this walk.

Walk past the last of the houses to the right to a kissing gate marked by a sign for a public footpath. Go through the gate and start climbing with a fence to the right and a slope covered by gorse to the left, passing a bench along the way. This good path continues climbing, seemingly aiming for a rocky break in the slope to the left with trees growing in it, until it suddenly swings left and continues climbing (a rougher path carries straight on: ignore this).

At the next dog-leg there is a choice once again. Swing right and keep climbing up to a viewpoint and another bench where there is a further split. Take the left-hand path, climbing onto a broad ridge with a rocky knoll at its far end. Before the knoll is reached there are two further splits. Keep left at the first and right at the second and climb up to the summit, from where there are splendid views.

Return by the same route.

Looking south over Ullapool

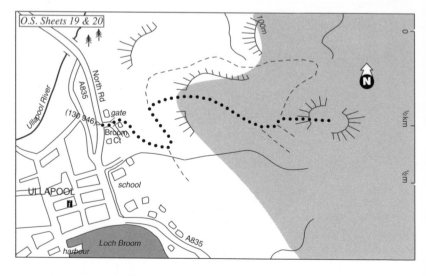

Distance: *6 miles/9.5km (there and back)*
Height climbed: *470m*
Difficulty: *Grade A*
Facilities: *Food (Dundonnell)*

A short moorland climb, along the floor of a narrow glen to a small lochan set in a corrie surrounded by rocky peaks and steep cliff faces. Paths rough and often unclear.

An Teallach is a rocky mass of ice-carved corries and buttresses, to the south of Dundonnell at the head of Little Loch Broom. To reach this walk, drive 1½ miles south of Dundonnell on the A832. There is a small lay-by shortly before the turn to Badrallach.

Cross the fence to the west (right-hand side) of the Coir' a' Ghiubhsachain Burn and follow the burn up the hill. This is tricky at first as there is a thick wood of pines and rhododendrons, but these gradually clear and the path is then marked by a series of cairns. Just beyond the edge of the wood there are a number of waterfalls. Above the falls the path runs along the side of the glen, through a landscape of glacial debris and deposits, peat bogs and exposed pavements of sandstone, before rising to the still grey waters of Loch Toll an Lochain. This is a most dramatic spot, set between the towering rocky spurs of An Teallach.

Return by the same route, keeping an eye open for wild goats along the way.

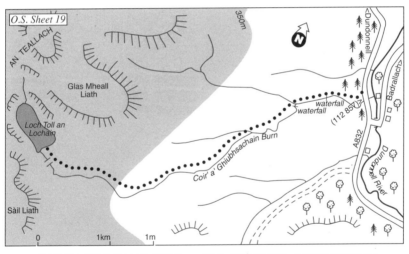

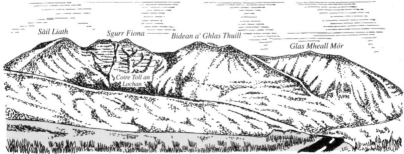

An Teallach from the south-east

Distance: *2 miles/3km (there and back)*
Height climbed: *270m*
Difficulty: *Grade B/C*
Facilities: *Food (Dundonnell)*

A steep climb up the slope to the south of Little Loch Broom, by the side of the spectacular Ardessie Falls, with excellent views and a possible extension. Paths faint but route obvious.

Ardessie is on the south side of Little Loch Broom, on the A832, 2¹/₂ miles west of Dundonnell. Driving from that direction, continue past the entrance to the fish farm (to the right) and park in the lay-by just beyond (to the left). Walk back down the road to where the Allt Airdeasaidh flows under the road and clamber up the rocks to the left of the burn.

There is a fall of some 40ft/12m just beyond the road, with a flat rock jutting over the edge and providing a fine viewpoint. Above this there is a fall of similar height, falling into a narrow gully, across the top of which a large boulder has been jammed. Beyond this there is a series of rapids and one broad, shimmering fall, dropping 30ft/9m into a wide basin, and above this a deep, narrow gorge lined with birch and Scots pine. Up this first stretch there are fine views northwards, across Little Loch Broom.

The path continues into the upper glen, with the bulk of Sgurr Ruadh dominating the skyline.

Ardessie Falls

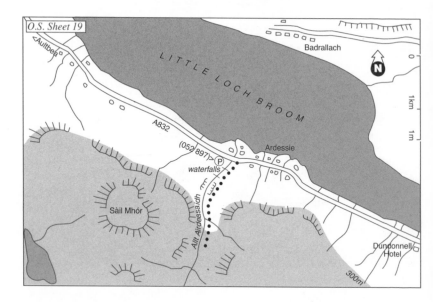

Distance: *4 miles/6.5km (there and back)*
Height climbed: *140m*
Difficulty: *Grade B*
Facilities: *Toilets, Food (Aultbea)*

A short, pleasant walk up a narrow glen with a waterfall at its head. Path rough but clear. Possible extension beyond the waterfall to the upper glen (some scrambling required). Good views.

S ix miles east of Aultbea the A832 curves round the head of Gruinard Bay, crossing three rivers. The middle of these three is Inverianvie River. Driving from Aultbea, the car park is just beyond the river, to the right of the road.

Start walking up the left-hand side of the river, along the foot of a narrow, rocky glen. The lower part of this route is a straight walk to a waterfall – visible from near the bottom of the glen. Beyond this fall the glen narrows to a shallow gorge full of rapids. Watch for a path starting to climb across the slope to the left before creeping along a narrow terrace beyond the head of the gorge. The glen eventually opens out into a wider valley, with the river meandering quietly through the deposits on the flat floor and steep hills rising on either side. The path continues to the head of the upper glen. Return by the same route.

On the opposite side of the road to the car park there are steep dunes, leading down to the wide sandy beaches of Gruinard Bay.

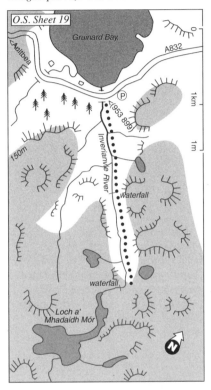

The glen of the Inverianvie River from the north

Distance: *6 miles/10km (there and back)*
Height climbed: *Negligible*
Difficulty: *Grade B/C*
Facilities: *Toilets, Food (Aultbea)*

A once metalled road, now gradually falling into disrepair, leading across rough moorland scattered with lochs to a ruined village above a sandy bay. Possible extension along coast.

Three miles north of Aultbea on the A832 is the tiny settlement of Laide. A narrow road turns off to the north here, signposted for Mellon Udrigle. Follow this road, with Gruinard Bay to your right, for 2 miles. A road cuts off to the left, signposted for Achgarve. Ignore this and continue until a second road heads off to the left, through a gate. Although metalled, this road is now in a bad state of repair and is no longer fit for any but the most rugged vehicles, so drive a short distance beyond the junction and park in the space to the right of the road.

Start walking along the old road, which rises gently by the side of a small burn, past little Loch na h-Innse Gairbhe, before dropping again, across the blanket of moorland heather, past Loch an t-Slagain to the deserted village of Slaggan; a few crumbling walls of which are still standing.

Below the village is narrow Slaggan Bay, surrounded by steep hills and cliffs and with a small sandy beach at its head. The bay opens on to the waters of the Minch, and looks west towards the Western Isles. Loch Ewe opens out just to the south.

A faint path wanders along the northern edge of the bay to the rocks at Gob a' Gheodha, and beyond towards Greenstone Point.

Ruin at Slaggan

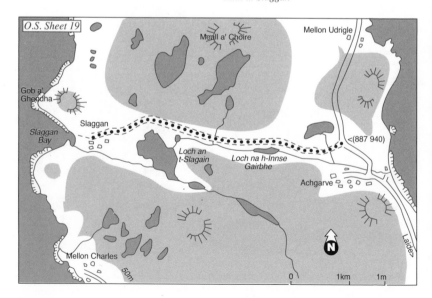

Distance: *2¹/₂ miles/4km*
Height climbed: *40m*
Difficulty: *Grade C*
Facilities: *Toilets, Food (Aultbea)*

A short loop through rough moorland behind low cliffs. Paths rough in places; views excellent. Cliff-top section unsuitable for small children if not kept under control at all times.

Two and a half miles north of Aultbea on the A832 is the settlement of Laide. Turn west from here onto the minor road signposted for Mellon Udrigle and follow it for three miles until the little township is reached. There is a small car park to the right of the road, in the dunes behind the sands of Camas a' Charraig.

Walk back to the road and turn right.

After a short distance the road cuts to the right and a rough vehicle track cuts off to the left. Follow this until it swings left towards a new house, then carry straight on along a rougher footpath through heather moorland.

The path drops down to a tiny estuary (crossable on a line of rocks when the tide is out) then swings right along the coast. The ground is rough and the paths faint, but there is little doubt of the route as you follow the rocky coast – rising to low cliffs in places – back round to the start.

Cliffs north of Mellon Udrigle

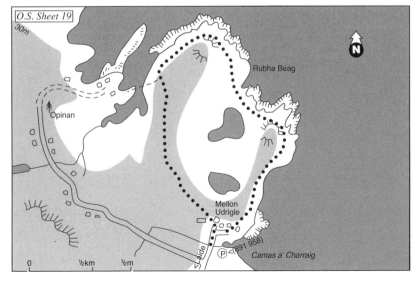

Distance: *5miles/8km*
Height climbed: *140m (from Tollie),*
230m (from Slattadale)
Difficulty: *Grade B*
Facilities: *Toilets (Slattadale);*
Food (Poolewe)

A rough but splendidly scenic footpath through lumpy, boggy, rocky moorland, giving fine views of Loch Maree (a large inland loch), its islands and the surrounding hills.

This route can be walked from either end, but it is easier, and the views are better, if started from Tollie. The car park for the northern end of the route is 1 mile south of Poolewe on the A832, almost opposite the entrance to Tollie Farm. At the other end of the route, there is a Forestry Commission car park at Slattadale, 8 miles south of Gairloch (or 13 miles south of Poolewe) on the same road. The walk cuts across a long loop in the road.

Starting from Tollie, walk a short distance down the A832 and turn left – the path is signposted. The early part of the route is across rough moorland, and a couple of small burns have to be crossed. The path gradually rises into a narrow pass, under the shadow of Creag Mhór Thollaidh. At the top of the pass, near the small loch, there is a view of the sea to the north. A little further on there

is an even better view to the south-east: looking down the length of Loch Maree, dotted with islands clothed with Scots pine. The slope of the northern shore is very steep and ends with the imposing mass of Slioch. The southern shore is less severe, but ends with the mass of peaks and buttresses around Beinn Eighe (Walk 11).

The path now drops to the boggy land by the side of the loch and enters the conifer plantations of Slattadale Forest. Follow a clear path – passing a low-level viewpoint overlooking the loch on the way – to the car park at Slattadale.

Islands on Loch Maree

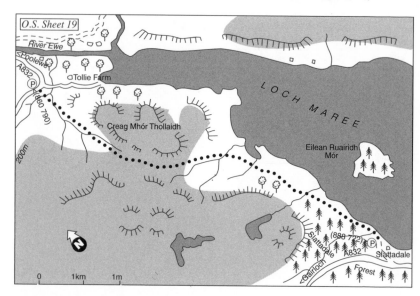

Leacanashie

Distance: 4¹/₂ miles/7km
Height climbed: 100m
Difficulty: Grade C
Facilities: Toilets (Lochcarron);
Food (Lochcarron)

A short, pleasant circuit... ninsula, passing throug... forest, but offering fine... rounding coastal scenery. ... but rough in places.

To reach Leacanashie take the small lochside road from Lochcarron. After about 3¹/₂ miles the road enters a wood. The walk starts up the slope opposite a small group of houses just beyond a cattle grid, and there is a small car park at the start of the path, to the right of the road. (If this is full, continue to the end of the road and park at Ardaneaskan, also on the route).

Cut up across an area of recently planted trees. The path is clear here, and soon joins a forestry track. After a short distance a rough footpath, marked by a small cairn, cuts off to the right of the main track, climbing across an area of recently replanted forest. Follow this path over a low watershed and down into the valley of the Reraig Burn.

When the path reaches a forest road, cut right. After a short distance there is a junction. Turn left, crossing the

burn. At the next junction keep to the left and follow the clear track past Reraig Cottage, along the edge of the tidal Loch Reraig then round the headland to Ardaneaskan. Follow the public road back to the start.

Strome Castle

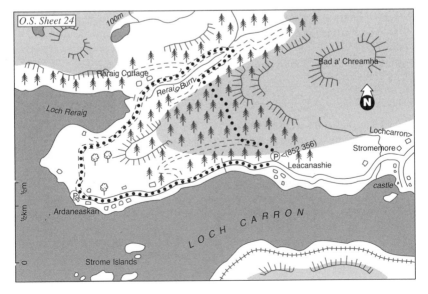

Distance: *1-4 miles/1.5-6.5km*
Height climbed: *up to 550m (long route)*
Difficulty: *Grade B/C*
Facilities: *Toilets (visitor centre),
Food (Kinlochewe)*

*Two waymarked walks: one a short loop
through mature Scots pine woodland; the
longer climbing above the trees to give
spectacular views of the surrounding
mountains. Paths rough in places.*

B einn Eighe is south-west of the
southern end of Loch Maree. The
car park for the nature trails is by the
side of the loch, 2¹/₂ miles north of Kinlochewe on the A832.

Beinn Eighe is a National Nature
Reserve, of interest due to both the pine
woodland of its lower slopes and its bare
summits. Information on the wildlife
and geology of the area is available
from the visitor centre (2 miles towards
Kinlochewe).

The two trails start by passing under
the road by the side of the burn which
passes the car park. Immediately
beyond the road the trails split: for the
short, woodland trail go right, across a
footbridge; for the longer, mountain trail
go straight on. The latter climbs above
the trees to a high plateau dotted with

lochans, providing splendid views. This
route is steep in places, and care must be
taken to follow the cairns which mark the
route.

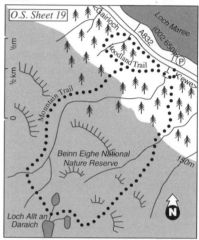

Lael Forest

*Two short, signposted walks on good
paths through largely coniferous woodland.*

Distance: *both walks ³/₄ mile/1km*
Height climbed: *40m*
Difficulty: *Grade C*
Facilities: *Toilets*

L ael Forest is on the steep slope
along the east side of the valley of
the River Broom. The two car parks are
10 miles south of Ullapool on the A835,
near the head of Loch Broom.

The two waymarked paths are largely
on forestry tracks, with some narrow
footpaths, and both are well signposted.
The forest includes a woodland garden,
with a wide selection of labelled coni-
fers and broad-leaved trees.

Corrieshalloch Gorge

*Two very short walks leading to view-
points overlooking a spectacular, deep,
wooded gorge (**NB:** please stick to paths).*

Distance: *up to ³/₄ mile/1km*
Height climbed: *up to 80m*
Difficulty: *Grade C*

T o reach Corrieshalloch Gorge, drive
south from Ullapool on the A835 for
10 miles to the junction with the A832.
Turn right here and park in the NTS car
park after ¹/₂ mile (fee).

Two paths leave the car park: the
shorter going right and dropping directly
to the suspension bridge over the gorge;
the longer following a path along the
gorge edge before cutting back to the
car park.